Tangled Vines

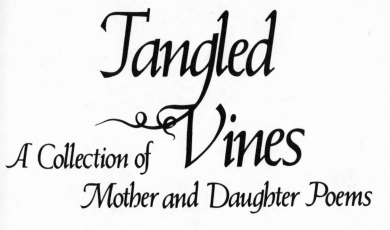

Tangled
Vines
A Collection of
Mother and Daughter Poems

Edited by Lyn Lifshin

BEACON PRESS ❦ BOSTON

Copyright © 1978 by Lyn Lifshin

Beacon Press books are published under the auspices
of the Unitarian Universalist Association

Published simultaneously in Canada by
Fitzhenry & Whiteside Limited, Toronto

Simultaneous publication in hardcover and paperback editions

All rights reserved

Printed in the United States of America

(hardcover)   9   8   7   6   5   4   3   2   1
(paperback)   9   8   7   6   5   4   3   2

Library of Congress Cataloging in Publication Data

Main entry under title:
Tangled vines.
   1. Mothers and daughters—Poetry.   2. American
poetry—Women authors.   3. American poetry—20th
century.   I. Lifshin, Lyn.
PS595.M65T3   811'.008'0352   77–88340
ISBN 0–8070–6366–5
ISBN 0–8070–6367–3 (pbk.)

Contents

Introduction

The relationship between a mother and her daughter is as
varied, as mysterious, as constantly changing and interconnected
as the patterns that touch, move away from, and touch again
in a kaleidoscope. It is the primary relationship between females
and, for many women, the most profound. Yet surprisingly
little notice has been taken of it. Perhaps this is because the
birth of a daughter has been seen as a kind of failure or disap-
pointment in our patriarchal society—something to be apolo-
gized for or, at best, accepted quietly until the birth of a son. As
Adrienne Rich writes in her chapter on motherhood and daughter-
hood in *Of Woman Born,* the mother-daughter relationship "has
been minimized and trivialized in the annals of patriarchy.
Whether in theological doctrine or art or sociology or psycho-
analytic theory, it is the mother and son who appear as the
eternal, determinative dyad. Small wonder, since theology, art,
and social theory have been produced by sons."

The mother-daughter relationship has been largely ignored
in literature. Yet some of the most moving poems written by
women are about their mothers and their daughters. Now, with
women reexamining their roles and the complexities of their
relationships, putting together a collection of mother and
daughter poems seemed especially intriguing to me. Poems like
Anne Sexton's "Pain for a Daughter," Shirley Kaufman's
"Mothers, Daughters," and Sylvia Plath's "The Disquieting
Muses" had made me want to do the book. I hoped the subject
would touch and intrigue people who might not ordinarily
read poetry.

When I first started soliciting manuscripts for this volume,
I wasn't sure what reaction to expect. The response was in-

stant and overwhelming. Sometimes thirty to forty (often huge) packets of poetry would arrive at my home in a single day. There were love poems, poems of hate and anger, poems of celebration, poems of disappointment.

Some of the themes were expected: the death of a mother; the birth of a child; poems about inheritance—inheritance of objects: dishes, linen; of physical traits: a certain bone structure or build; and emotional inheritance: fear, guilt, dependence. There were poems about rituals; about lust, envy, and rivalry; about separation, estrangement, and letting go; about acceptance, rejection, and reconciliation; poems with recurring images— hooks, fish, and soup; claws, cats, and hands. Other themes surprised me more: "The daughter I don't have," and the feelings of guilt, abnormality, longing, and loss—of having a hole where a daughter should be.

In some poems the mother merged with the lover; others froze some small past moment, a chunk of time, like something caught in a photograph. Many were about the need for closeness, the fear of closeness or suffocation; some were about being one's mother and the fear of becoming her—the need to be different, opposite, the need to revolt. A few poems switched the mother and daughter around, exploring the question of who was mothering whom; others were about the need for approval, the lack of approval.

Several poems mixed attraction and repulsion, denial and nostalgia. Few idealized the relationship without touching on feelings of ambivalence, fear, and panic—the nightmare of loving or being loved too much, the nightmare of being loved or loving too little.

This collection reflects the range of feelings and emotions that exist between a mother and her daughter—the joys, the guilt, the anguish, the fears. It is meant to be a celebration of this relationship. Reading these poems, I realized that feelings I thought only I felt are shared. I hope you'll find that, too.

Lyn Lifshin   Niskayuna, New York

Tangled Vines

Rachel
(Rachel [rā′chal], a ewe)

We named you
for the sake
of the syllables
and for the small boat
that followed the *Pequod,*
gathering lost children
of the sea.

We named you
for the dark-eyed girl
who waited at the well
while her lover
worked seven years
and again
seven.

We named you
for the small daughters
of the Holocaust
who followed their six-pointed stars
to death
and were all of them
known as
Rachel.

Linda Pastan

from ℐhree Women

I see her in my sleep, my red, terrible girl.
She is crying through the glass that separates us.
She is crying, and she is furious.
Her cries are hooks that catch and grate like cats.
It is by these hooks she climbs to my notice.
She is crying at the dark, or at the stars
That at such a distance from us shine and whirl.

I think her little head is carved in wood,
A red, hard wood, eyes shut and mouth wide open.
And from the open mouth issue sharp cries
Scratching at my sleep like arrows,
Scratching at my sleep, and entering my side.
My daughter has no teeth. Her mouth is wide.
It utters such dark sounds it cannot be good.

Sylvia Plath

Her Sleep

Wasps or hornets rattle on the sills
and fill the vestibule with danger;
my daughter, rocked by lullabies
of wind, naps inside mosquito netting
like a bride before the veil is lifted
for the rough world to injure with its kiss.
Still a wound my husband cannot enter
since the child departed from me—her dream
drags its belly, suns on a honeyed spoon—
seeing her sleep, I am stung.

Jill Hoffman

Thoughts About My Daughter Before Sleep

1

Ariel, one true
Miracle of my life, my golden
Sparrow, burning in your crib
As the rain falls over the meadow
And the squirrel corn,
While the fragrant hyacinth
Sleeps in its bed in the rich
Mud of the North, while foamflowers
Climb through small arches of rain, and the sun
Brings lilies and dark blue berries
In cluster, leaf on leaf again,
I wonder how I came to give you life.

2

Here, where the twisted stalks
Of deer grass zigzag
Branches from the tree, where
Honeysuckles trumpet, "All joy
Is in the dark vessels of the skin!"
And thorn apples open their leaves,
I marvel to have made you perfect
As a small plant, you, filled
Up with sunlight and
Fragrant as ferns.

3

And before snow
Covers ivy and bluet
Shall I teach you this old
Summer's lesson
About seeds? About miracles
Of growth? Here are the bursting zinnias,
Asters, prongs
Of phlox—shall I wake you?
Take you out of sleep
And roll you in the apple fields?

4

And through you
I am born as I lie down
In the seedbox of my own beginnings,
Opening the wild part of me,
Once lost once lost
As I was breathing
In the vines of childhood.

Sandra Hochman

Telemann
To A.C.

Measure is a guess the mind makes about itself:
gestures and glimpses worked into confidence.

My daughter is excessive in her small age,
takes in the world like breakfast,
pricks the raw yolks of mornings
till they run like blood in her mouth.
Skin's a cage, or a fiction.
Names prowl in the tall grass, beasts
tamed into syllables:
cat's-paw, foxglove, hart's-tongue.
Birds have gone south three times and come back.
She serves up fistfuls of powdered rock
to the sea, equitably pours hope
at the sand's perpetual teatime.

In music things begin and end,
spread, strain, and return into themselves,
are contained: behave well,
like lessons we have learned and been praised for.
Untutored in these comforts, my girl
has her small ways.

Helen Chasin

To My Four-Year-Old Daughter

I lost my temper twice today,
Once when you ordered me around like a maid,
And once when you picked all the unripe plums
      from our tree.
You said I yelled so much it made you sleepy,
Popped in your thumb and drifted away.
Then, imagining you sad, I felt guilty.
You, my firstborn child, my beautiful girl.
Remember when your ear hurt and we rocked all night.
How many hours, awake, I stared in your face
Seeing prongs that reach
Deep in your childhood, deep in mine.

Gail Todd

Waiting for the Transformation

My daughter is a mystic about cats.
I am afraid. I have seen her conversing with them,
watched her nod, blink her eyes; and the cats
twitch their whiskers, almost smile.
When she was five, she told me that if our old Tom
curled close to the fire, there would be
snow the next day. Often there was.

I think, although I fear to know for certain,
that she becomes a cat at night.
Just yesterday, I saw tiger shadows
on the wall of her room. I hear strange cries
in the house before dawn, feel the rattle of purrs,
a softness that feathers my face.

I do not think about it, tell no one.
I have decided to wait until other children's eyes
glint fire, until they all leave their mothers' arms
and turn wild—howling in the night.

Judith Minty

My Daughter's Ring

A ring of fear
through the nose
yanks her from a dream,
pulls her to the bathroom
mirror where she sees
a thin silver wire
piercing her nostrils,
its metallic perfume
jolting her like ammonia,
as invisible threads
shoot from the ring,
slip down her throat
and wind around her stomach
tighter, tighter,
until she bends
in the sick smell of night
to vomit, sensing,
even at six,
that the ring will grow
as she grows
and will always fit—perfectly.

Barbara Eve

*W*hat My Child Learns of the Sea

What my child learns of the sea
of the summer thunders
of the riddles that hide in the curve of spring
she will learn in my twilights
and childlike
revise every autumn

What my child learns
as her winters grow into time
has ripened in my own body
to enter her eyes with first light.

This is why
more than blood
or the milk I have given
one day a strange girl will step
to the back of a mirror
cutting my ropes
of sea and thunder and spring.
Of the way she will taste her autumns—
toast-brittle or warmer than sleep—
and the words she will use for winter
I stand already condemned

Audre Lorde

Mothers, Daughters

Through every night we hate,
preparing the next day's
war. She bangs the door.
Her face laps up my own
despair, the sour, brown eyes,
the heavy hair she won't
tie back. She's cruel,
as if my private meanness
found a way to punish us.
We gnaw at each other's
skulls. Give me what's mine.
I'd haul her back, choking
myself in her, herself
in me. There is a book
called *Poisons* on her shelf.
Her room stinks with incense,
animal turds, hamsters
she strokes like silk. They
exercise on the bathroom
floor, and two drop through
the furnace vent. The whole
house smells of the accident,
the hot skins, the small
flesh rotting. Six days
we turn the gas up then
to fry the dead. I'd fry
her head if I could until
she cried love, love me!

All she won't let me do.
Her stringy figure in
the windowed room shares
its thin bones with no one.
Only her shadow on the glass
waits like an older sister.
Now she stalks, leans forward,
concentrates merely on getting
from here to there. Her feet
are bare. I hear her breathe
where I can't get in. If I
break through to her, she will
drive nails into my tongue.

Shirley Kaufman

Aubade

In the early morning
I shake my head
to clear away the static
of the dream
the way my daughter
shakes the radio she holds
against her ear
as if it were a shell.
On the table between us
the sun spreads
its slow stain;
fog lifts
from the coffee;
a heart drifts out of reach
on the surface
of the milk.
Now my daughter takes the day
into her hand
like fresh baked bread—
she offers me a piece.

Linda Pastan

Pain for a Daughter

Blind with love, my daughter
has cried nightly for horses,
those long-necked marchers and churners
that she has mastered, any and all,
reigning them in like a circus hand—
the excitable muscles and the ripe neck;
tending this summer, a pony and a foal.
She who is too squeamish to pull
a thorn from the dog's paw,
watched her pony blossom with distemper,
the underside of the jaw swelling
like an enormous grape.
Gritting her teeth with love,
she drained the boil and scoured it
with hydrogen peroxide until pus
ran like milk on the barn floor.

Blind with loss all winter,
in dungarees, a ski jacket and a hard hat,
she visits the neighbors' stable,
our acreage not zoned for barns;
they who own the flaming horses
and the swan-whipped thoroughbred
that she tugs at and cajoles,
thinking it will burn like a furnace
under her small-hipped English seat.

Blind with pain she limps home.
The thoroughbred has stood on her foot.
He rested there like a building.

He grew into her foot until they were one.
The marks of the horseshoe printed
into her flesh, the tips of her toes
ripped off like pieces of leather,
three toenails swirled like shells
and left to float in blood in her riding boot.

Blind with fear, she sits on the toilet,
her foot balanced over the washbasin,
her father, hydrogen peroxide in hand,
performing the rites of the cleansing.
She bites on a towel, sucked in breath,
sucked in and arched against the pain,
her eyes glancing off me where
I stand at the door, eyes locked
on the ceiling, eyes of a stranger,
and then she cries . . .
Oh my God, help me!
Where a child would have cried *Mama!*
Where a child would have believed *Mama!*
she bit the towel and called on God
and I saw her life stretch out . . .
I saw her torn in childbirth,
and I saw her, at that moment,
in her own death and I knew that she
knew.

Anne Sexton

Letters to My Daughters #3

Your great-grandfather dreamed that his son
would be an engineer, the old man,
the blacksmith with square hands.
To the Finns up north in that snow country
engineer was like doctor today. In the forties
in Detroit, I learned to play the violin.
So did my father when he was a boy in Ishpeming.
He and I never spoke about becoming. Our conversation
was my bow slipping over the strings, my fingers
searching for notes to tell him, his foot tapping time.
That violin cracked ten years ago, it dried out
from loneliness in the coat closet.
Your grandfather, the engineer, sometimes plays his
at night behind a closed kitchen door.
Your grandmother sews and turns up the television.
But what of you two? The piano you practiced over
is still here, a deaf mute in our living room.
I strike an imperfect chord now and remember
we never spoke of what was dreamed for you.

Judith Minty

Fish Story

The mother watched her daughter kneeling
slowly into the green-silver
seamless gel of tub-water,
those thighs like two fish, that whole
glazed torso like a fish, the firm
slit a noncommittal fish mouth
smiling neither way, seeming to
sip the water and dip under
down to the navel eye—she could almost
see the scales on this mermaid, this sleek
stretching child, this glittering eel
who used to be a shrimp in her sea—
this woman she once had firmly in her body—

this is the fact she is supposed to forget,
the mother eyeballing this slick girl,
this replica, this split-finned tail
thrashing white in the tub, this fish
that got away.

Sharon Olds

Circus Song
for Susan and Valerie Beere

Dear, you are in my hands like dough. Twisting
And turning, how
Can I get you free of me?

In the muffled agony of the pillow
Face down, beating it,
I know

For every step forward you take
Three backward and blame me.

Little yeasty thing
You call me animal trainer, insist

I keep you in the same cage
I'm trying to get you out of:

Talking all day long,
Backwards and forwards you keep pacing

Like a hungry cat in a circus
Over my bones you crack the whip

And then weep for it, the guilt
Just sticky enough to keep you

Right where you want to be, trapped
Trying out your weapons but safe,
Wrapped in your warm coverings until you rise

Dear clown, dear savage daughter
So different from me and yet
So much like me I know

No matter how much it hurts
Sharpening your claws on me first
Is how you begin to grow.

Patricia Goedicke

The Mountain

1

In the morning I am alone in the icy room
everyone has gone to climb the mountain
the only sound is the noise in my head
machine of my anger or my fear
that won't shut off
the wind keeps cranking it.

My daughter has fled to the mountain
a piece of her dress in my hand
it is green
and I hold it next to my ear
to stop the wind.

What she took out of me
was not what I meant to give.
She hears strange voices.
I dream she's the child I grew up with
kneeling beside her hamsters
soft things she cared for
cradling them in her hands.

I want to make my words into a hamster
and nest them in her palms
to be sorry again
when she falls out of the tree
and breaks her arms.

She runs to an empty house
with her own prophets

they sit shoulder to shoulder
waiting for the sky to open
they can already see through a tiny crack
where the path begins.

2

Yesterday we saw how roots of mangroves
suck the warm sea at the desert's edge
and keep the salt
the leaves are white
and flaky as dead skin.
My ankles swell.
I must be drowning in my own brine.

A Bedouin woman stands veiled
in the ruined courtyard
there's a well
a hole in the ground
where she leads the camel by a rope
I watch her fill the bucket
and the camel drinks
lifting its small shrewd head
rinsing its teeth with a swollen tongue.

The woman is covered in black
her body her head her whole face black
except for the skin around her eyes.

My daughter watches me watch her
with the same eyes.

She picks up a handful of rocks
and hits the camel

shrieking she strikes it
over and over to make it move.

I am alone in the icy room
everyone has gone to climb the mountain
the only sound is the woman
chasing the camel with the rocks.

I look out at the dry riverbed.
I let her go.

Shirley Kaufman

Making the Jam Without You
for Judy

Old daughter, small traveler
asleep in a German featherbed
under the eaves in a postcard town
of turrets and towers,
I am putting a dream in your head.

Listen! Here it is afternoon.
The rain comes down like bullets.
I stand in the kitchen,
that harem of good smells
where we have bumped hips and
cracked the cupboards with our talk
while the stove top danced with pots
and it was not clear who did
the mothering. Now I am
crushing blackberries
to make the annual jam
in a white cocoon of steam.

Take it, my sleeper. Redo it
in any of your three
languages and nineteen years.
Change the geography.
Let there be a mountain,
the fat cows on it belled
like a cathedral. Let
there be someone beside you
as you come upon the ruins
of a schloss, all overgrown
with a glorious thicket,

its brambles soft as wool.
Let him bring the buckets
crooked on his angel arms
and may the berries, vaster
than any forage in
the mild hills of New Hampshire,
drop in your pail, plum size,
heavy as the eyes
of an honest dog
and may you bear them
home together to a square
white unreconstructed kitchen
not unlike this one.

Now may your two heads
touch over the kettle,
over the blood of the berries
that drink up sugar and sun,
over that tar-thick boil
love cannot stir down.
More plainly than
the bric-a-brac of shelves
filling with jelly glasses,
more surely than
the light driving through them
trite as rubies, I see him
as pale as paraffin beside you.
I see you cutting
fresh baked bread to spread it
with the bright royal fur.

At this time
I lift the flap of your dream
and slip out thinner than a sliver
as your two mouths open
for the sweet stain of purple.

Maxine Kumin

Scenario

My parents stand by my bed.
They look down, talking
about how I am growing before their eyes.

They watch as my hair
darkens and curls, as my milk teeth
fall out and new ones appear.

They barely blink when the rings
of my nipples rise like blown bubbles
and soft hair tops the vee of my legs.

They step back when a boy
joins me in bed and we kiss,
touching with tentative fingers.

They stand in the doorway
as the boy grows into a man and we kiss
harder, our bodies twisting into a braid.

They stare from the hallway
as my belly swells like a blister.
They fade back when I start labor.

I stand by her bed
seeing her grow before my eyes.
I step back.

Barbara Eve

The Second Heart

The child I do not have
is the one my mother
always wanted. Every holiday
she asks what I have named it.

This child is like no other;
it will not hide in my belly
like a lodged bullet, pulling
the walls down around it.

It will not flower
in my mouth or cling
like a barnacle to my wooden
hip. It will not be my gift.

We will not speak of miracles.
We will not lay your head
on my lap listening
for my second heartbeat

that is half yours.
There will be no paper doll
connections to send electricity
through the family.

But the child I do not have
will not be forgotten.
It hangs around my neck,
a heavy locket,

protecting me. I hear it
crying from a place inside
and I speak in tongues
only my mother understands.

It knows how old I am.
Each birthday now
I take away one candle
for the baby.

And you see the secret
in my hands, how they shake
when I undress,
when I make up the bed.

The child I do not have
rides on your shoulders
when we go out walking.
Everyone we pass notices.

Ellen Wittlinger

ℱlowers

Changing water. Adding aspirin. Nitrogen, potash or
sugar (white) to keep limpness from descending
upon these purple and magenta asters with broad golden centers
and petals packed in two rows making fringe above
green spread leaves, still alive. Keep cutting stems
to retain the vertical pull of water up into
the barely charged life.

She said there was a tiny charge of energy still, like a cord,
    moving between
me and the child—a girl—though its body life had stopped after
    four months,
only one leg intact on the fetus. "It's better," the doctor said.
    "Nature
knows best," he said, at the end.

That was ten years ago. He was pulling me along on an immacu-
    late silver table,
larger than a serving tray, I thought, sheet over me then, white
    linen, and
their faces soothing. Shapes of words and eyes. I couldn't
    identify. Something
inside me had broken, though I tried to hold it in. Red, on
    everything.

In the white stone pitcher I always place flowers.
First water, then the spiked metal frog
where each flower is stuck in arrangements of
height, darkness or intensity of bloom. The accidents
interest me. The Japanese effect of less.
Space showing its wandering shape between leaves
and the sudden curve of a stem
dying slowly towards what light is
in the room. One forgets about hunger,
absorbed in the fuchsia and the mauve.

Kathleen Fraser

from Changing

I was born in a small hospital in Tokyo. Mamma says she remembers two things:

A mouse running across the floor, which she took as a sign of good luck.

A nurse bending down and whispering apologetically: "I'm afraid it's a girl. Would you prefer to inform your husband yourself?"

Liv Ullmann

The Petals of the Tulips

The petals of the tulips
just before they open

when they're pulling
the last dark purple energy through the stem

are covered with a whitish veil,
a caul.

I like them best then:

they're me the month before I was born

the month Mother spent
flat on her back in the hospital.

The way I found out—

once, in round eight of one of our fights
I hissed at her, "I didn't ask to be born!"

and she threw back her head and howled,
remembering,

"You? You?

Hot as it was that summer
I had to lie there for weeks
hanging on to you.

You? You were begging to be born!"

Judith Hemschemeyer

$\mathcal{F}$or My Mother's Mother

Driving with my mother
from Chicago to Boston,
only ourselves to talk to.
In a snow storm between Buffalo and Syracuse
she told me quietly
how her mother died.

I was eight and Lorraine was four.
Lorraine was a difficult child.
We moved a lot because of Daddy's job
but he had finally promised Mother they would settle.
They built a home in the country
with window seats and flagstone fireplace.
We moved in.
Three weeks later Daddy's company wanted him to move again.
He went.
Mother was going to pack and follow.
But Lorraine was a difficult child
and Mother was pregnant again.
She couldn't face moving and having another child
so she went to her mother and aunt.
Grandma Andersen told her something,
gave her something,
I don't know,
from the old country.
It didn't work.
She was sick.
I heard her screams from the next room
but they wouldn't let me go in.
By the time Daddy got home she was dead.

He never knew what happened or how she died.
What do you mean, I asked?
How could he not know?
Didn't he care? Didn't he ask?
They just told him it was a woman's problem.
He never knew. After he died
Grandma Andersen told Lorraine and she told me.
All I remembered was the house
where my mother died
and how she cried
and they finally took Lorraine and me away
so we wouldn't hear.

For two years now
I have heard my mother's mother's screams.
They are all I know of her
they are with me.
I have listened to her screams
as they became my own.
I have lived through her death.
Untold, yet I know how she did it.
She took some poison
when that didn't work
she shoved something up her vagina.
And that worked and she bled
and expelled and was infected
and poisoned and she died.
I have heard her screams of pain
splutter through her clenched teeth
and grow weaker.
I have heard her screams of rage
deep in my chest

as she cursed her husband
and her mother
and Lorraine who was always a difficult child
and herself who could not cope,
who should have been different
or better
or more able to manage these things somehow.

I asked, a year later: what was her name?
Whose?
Your mother, my grandmother,
what was her name?
Judith, she said.
I named my first daughter after my mother.

Judith McDaniel

from ## Good Times

My Mama moved among the days
like a dreamwalker in a field;
seemed like what she touched was hers
seemed like what touched her couldn't hold,
she got us almost through the high grass
then seemed like she turned around and ran
right back in
right back on in

Lucille Clifton

For My Mother

I am afraid to begin this poem.
I take a walk to the mailbox. I make a cup of tea.
I call opening lines into my head. None have power.
All the poems I've written of Dad, Herb, lovers—
and you, the one person I trust to love me, to be there for me,
    as long as you live, you, I don't know how to write to .

There is so much I could say to you, so much I feel for you,
so intimately my life is bound with yours, my life is yours,
this way we go beyond time, this way we are all of who we have
    been, will be, at once.
I think of Anne Sexton's words: "A woman *is* her mother.
                    That's the main thing."

I am you.
And so, there is nothing I can say about my feelings for you,
    nothing I can think of you that's simple.
Too closely am I mixed with everything I see.

Sometimes I look in the mirror and see in my mouth the same
    taut line I saw in yours
the day I came home and said I was going to Canada with a man.
I will never forget the way you stood, washing dishes, placing
    them on the soft towel,
crying and telling me all day you'd been counting out wrong
    change for the customers, you'd buttoned your sweater
    askew.
I went to the bathroom and brought you back Kleenex, a pale
    gray-green Kleenex.

"With a strange man," you kept repeating.
I told you I wouldn't go and went secretly.

I find myself leaning my head on my hand, watching to see if
    someone will walk through the gate.
I don't want to be disturbed.
The thread I feel between this flow of words and me is tenuous,
    anything could break it, and so much I want to say these
    things.

Our bodies—we have the same full breasts, the same well-
    shaped legs, even at sixty you have well-shaped legs.
The same potbelly, small hips, pelvis tilted back, protecting our
    sex.
Every morning I do yoga now. I do backbends. I rotate my hips,
    listening to the bones crack into unfamiliar positions.
I am trying to break our structure, to stop walking with my
    chin thrust forward, my shoulders hunched up to my ears—
    how you always admired long graceful necks.
Is it possible? Is it possible that years from now my body will
    look less like yours?
How much leeway do I have to become myself?

Mother, there have been times when I've looked at your mar-
    riage with Dad and I've thought you wasted yourself,
you would've been happier with a man more full of joy, not a
    sick man,
someone who would've taught you the lindy, taken you sailing
    in a panama, pinched your behind while you scrambled the
    eggs.
And sometimes I've thought you beat him down, out-talked him,
    out-worked him, out-loved him till he just stopped trying.

And mostly, I know none of this is true, or it's all true, but so
    is everything else,
and I'm just afraid of the ways I'll choose my own life, the limits
    I'll set, the habits I won't give up.

Can you understand this? Is it too painful to read?
Last year when I gave you my book, you told me you weren't
    ready to talk about it.
Can we never talk about these things?
Oh, when Alan and I had stopped making love and I turned the
    living room upside down at least a couple times a week,
    crawled under the covers and screamed until he'd drive
    away, leaving Sunshine confused on the porch—
Mother, I wanted to call you and say, "Did this happen to you?
    Did you live through it? What is it in me—you *know* me—
    what is it that's making me like this, what is it I bring on
    myself?"
Am I so afraid my life will be like I imagine yours—warm, but
    not sexual; caring, but without passion?
Am I so afraid that I'm making it happen like that for myself?
Or are the patterns too strong to break anyway?
Tell me I'm wrong. Tell me you loved to make love.
Tell me I don't have to be afraid at how much I'm like you.

Oh Mother, when I think of you reading this, I feel wrong.
What right do I have to drag you through all my struggles?
And besides, you've been through your own. Isn't once enough?
With the sun shining on the wet bark of the redwoods and Sun-
    shine biting at his fleas,
with the avocado growing like a beanstalk, not even I feel like
    wading through it all.
Sometimes I think I think too much.

The coils of my heater, glowing like a jack-o'-lantern, remind
    me of something you once said.
It was one of those days when I was 12 or 13 and combing my
    hair in the powder room mirror, crying at the big mass of
    frizz, so unlike Judy Lockitch's silky flip.
Usually at times like this you knew enough to stay out of the
    way, knew anything you said would only make it worse,
but that day you must've had a clue that I needed something,
    needed you, and you said, "You won't always feel like this.
    Someday it won't matter."
I stopped crying and looked at you. "When?"
"I don't know," you told me, "but someday you won't care that
    you have curly hair."
I believed you. You were right.

I believed everything you said. I almost always obeyed.
Except around sex, which I hid, as I thought I sensed you ask
    me to.
That was the only place I cut myself away.
But I needed you—
with my recurrent cystitis and my mounting fear of that burning
    pee nothing seemed to cure for long,
with the knife-happy doctor in Baltimore who wouldn't even
    come to the emergency room when I was carried in—tubes
    clotted and about to burst—by a nice man passing by the
    hospital,
with the home-town boy returned from war who passed me
    gonorrhea in the front seat of his parents' car, hoping to
    give me a baby, even if I *was* on the pill—because he loved
    me so much (but not enough to drop a postcard telling me
    to check for clap). I carried *that* baby six months before I
    knew.

Momma, I began to think I really was sickly.
Momma, I needed to talk to you.

Momma—I've never called you Momma.
Mommy, when I was little. Mom, and Mother.
Who is this Momma arising here? this woman I could have
    talked to.

Does it sound like I'm accusing you?
Of course. And yet, I don't feel accusing at all right now. I
    don't even feel critical.
I'm not afraid today of being like you. I like you.
It's good to talk to you. Even if this hurts you, it's good to talk
    to you.
I don't think, deep down, you really want to be estranged from
    me, really want me to keep so much to myself.
At least not all the time, not without the door opening once in
    a while and the closed-off words rushing out.
Or, if you really don't want to know, then you're going to have
    to tell me right out.
I'm not going to keep assuming it. I might be wrong.

What more is there to say?
Aready the sun is going behind the trees.
This summer I thought you might be dying.
None of this made much difference then.
I remember the Wednesday I called you to get the first word
    from the doctor.
Friends were here for the afternoon. We were down by the river,
    skipping stones.
At five I came back to the house and called.

When I heard the good news—even that tentative good news—
    I ran to the river calling out, "She's going to be okay.
    It's okay."
Everyone was glad and they asked some questions, then seemed
    to forget.
I returned to the house just to sit with the news, sit with you,
    for a blissful while, giving thanks.

Oh Mom, live a long time. At least as long as Grandmom, longer
    if you can and keep your health.
We're building a community here. A place with lots of room.
Somewhere you could even live if you ever can't make meals for
    yourself or do your little bit of cleaning up.
But that's a long way off. I only wanted to let you know I won't
    forget you.

After saying all these hard things, there's a voice in me urging,
    "Tell her about the good things. Tell her what you ap-
    preciate."
And I could go on and on about the way you let me make my
    own decisions, run my own affairs, never were stupid like
    Marilyn's mother, telling her she couldn't take art,
the way you never minded if I left my shoes in the living room
    and you washed out my stockings just to do for me.
You let me go to the beauty parlor with the other girls even
    though you knew it was too soon,
and you never set much stock in getting rich, or being first
    in the class, or famous,
never made me have table manners, say please or thank you, just
    to look good, or go to synagogue, or say that I believed
    in God.

And I remember how you held me and called him a bastard when
the delivery man forced his tongue into my child mouth,
and the time I couldn't go to girl scout camp you let me spend
the whole ten dollars *any* way I wanted. I bought a doll
dress for $7.50—and that was 1956.

When it snowed, you shoveled out the car, and you could drive
like a trucker and swing cases of beer onto the counter.
All the customers loved you. The old caddy Roger called you
Mom and held up his huge fist, showing over and over
what he'd do if anybody ever tried to hurt you.
And you had the guts to play the numbers, the horses, and the
stock market—I remember how you held Sunshine Mining
for years because you liked the name.

But most of all is the way you loved me, loved me like I want to
love and rarely can,
loved me with the feeling that nothing I could ever do,
no way I could ever be,
nothing that might happen in this world
could lessen, could change, how much you love me.

I am crying as I write this, Momma.
This time the Momma sounds right.
It is my grown-up woman's way of saying Mommy, my name of
endearment,
to tell you I am grateful for how much you have loved me,
I am grateful that through your love, you taught me love,
and I am grateful to have this feeling welling up in me,
Mother, Mommy, Momma, Mom—I love you.

Ellen Bass

My Mother's Novel

Married academic woman ten
years younger holding that microphone
like a bazooka, forgive
me that I do some number of things
that you fantasize but frame
impossible. Understand:
I am my mother's daughter,
a small woman of large longings.

Energy hurled through her
confined and fierce as in a wind
tunnel. Born to a mean
harried poverty crosshatched
by spidery fears and fitfully
lit by the explosions
of politics, she married her way
at length into the solid working class:
a box of house, a car she could
not drive, a TV set kept turned
to the blare of football,
terrifying power tools, used wall
to wall carpeting protected
by scatter rugs.

Out of backyard posies
permitted to fringe
the proud hanky lawn
her imagination hummed
and made honey,

occasionally exploding
in mad queen swarms.

I am her only novel.
The plot is melodramatic,
hot lovers leap out of
thickets, it makes you cry
a lot, in between the revolutionary
heroics and making good
home-cooked soup.
Understand: I am my mother's
novel daughter: I
have my duty to perform.

Marge Piercy

The Disquieting Muses

Mother, mother, what illbred aunt
Or what disfigured and unsightly
Cousin did you so unwisely keep
Unasked to my christening, that she
Sent these ladies in her stead
With heads like darning-eggs to nod
And nod and nod at foot and head
And at the left side of my crib?

Mother, who made to order stories
Of Mixie Blackshort the heroic bear,
Mother, whose witches always, always
Got baked into gingerbread, I wonder
Whether you saw them, whether you said
Words to rid me of those three ladies
Nodding by night around my bed,
Mouthless, eyeless, with stitched bald head.

In the hurricane, when father's twelve
Study windows bellied in
Like bubbles about to break, you fed
My brother and me cookies and Ovaltine
And helped the two of us to choir:
"Thor is angry: boom boom boom!
Thor is angry: we don't care!"
But those ladies broke the panes.

When on tiptoe the schoolgirls danced,
Blinking flashlights like fireflies
And singing the glowworm song, I could
Not lift a foot in the twinkle-dress

But, heavy-footed, stood aside
In the shadow cast by my dismal-headed
Godmothers, and you cried and cried:
And the shadow stretched, the lights went out.

Mother, you sent me to piano lessons
And praised my arabesques and trills
Although each teacher found my touch
Oddly wooden in spite of scales
and the hours of practicing, my ear
Tone-deaf and yes, unteachable.
I learned, I learned, I learned elsewhere,
From muses unhired by you, dear
    mother,

I woke one day to see you, mother,
Floating above me in bluest air
On a green balloon bright with a million
Flowers and bluebirds that never were
Never, never, found anywhere.
But the little planet bobbed away
Like a soap-bubble as you called: Come here!
And I faced my traveling companions.

Day now, night now, at head, side, feet,
They stand their vigil in gowns of stone,
Faces blank as the day I was born,
Their shadows long in the setting sun
That never brightens or goes down.
And this is the kingdom you bore me to,
Mother, mother. But no frown of mine
Will betray the company I keep.

Sylvia Plath

My Mother Tries to Visit Me in the Dead of Night

I turn on all the lights.
I am never without electricity.
There was a girl who found a branch
from an Elder tree. She
said it was her
key
      and she walked in the thin radiance of
      a gold beater of stemwear
      and fresh Mosels.
But she was the girl I hated.
And I locked her up in the barn with the imaginary wild
horses.
Tap.
That is a branch scratching the window pane
a little wind out there
rocking the trees. My mother
looks in the window.
I know she is three thousand miles away
and I have imagined her face
out there.
Tap.
She rubs her fingers against the glass
and a moth flies off the ceiling. It would like to be
covered
with blood.
I feel that in bed I cannot stir
for the horrors around me: I forget that somewhere
there is you,
a man I love. My memory deserts me or locks you in a tool
shed, somewhere inaccessible,
somewhere beyond the sound of my voice.

My mother tries to visit me in the dead night
and her voice, her face,
are the trees I am so afraid to walk/ among

Diane Wakoski

$\mathcal{M}$other

Ash falls on the roof
of my house.

I have cursed you enough
in the lines of my poems
& between them,
in the silences which fall
like ash-flakes
on the watertank
from a smog-bound sky.

I have cursed you
because I remember
the smell of *Joy*
on a sealskin coat
& because I feel
more abandoned than a baby seal
on an ice floe red
with its mother's blood.

I have cursed you
as I walked & prayed
on a concrete terrace
high above the street
because whatever I pulled down
with my bruised hand
from the bruising sky,
whatever lovely plum
came to my mouth

you envied
& spat out.

Because you saw me in your image,
because you favored me,
you punished me.

It was only a form of you
my poems were seeking.
Neither of us knew.

For years
we lived together
in a single skin.

We shared fur coats.
We hated each other
as the soul hates the body
for being weak,
as the mind hates the stomach
for needing food,
as one lover hates the other.

I kicked
in the pouch of your theories
like a baby kangaroo.

I believed you
on Marx, on Darwin,
on Tolstoy & Shaw.
I said I loved Pushkin
(you loved him).

I vowed Monet
was better than Bosch.

Who cared?

I would have said nonsense
to please you
& frequently did.

This took the form,
of course,
of fighting you.

We fought so gorgeously!

We fought like one boxer
& his punching bag.
We fought like mismatched twins.
We fought like the secret sharer
& his shade.

Now we're apart.
Time doesn't heal
the baby to the womb.
Separateness is real
& keeps on growing.

One by one the mothers
drop away,
the lovers leave,
the babies outgrow clothes.

Some get insomnia—
the poet's disease—
& sit up nights
nursing
at the nipples
of their pens.

I have made hot milk
& kissed you where you are.
I have cursed my curses.
I have cleared the air.
& now I sit here writing,
breathing you.

Erica Jong

Daughterly

So many women, writing,
escaped their mothers—
mine, in her nightgown,
retreated into a wordless depression.

If only I could have
spoken for her,
but she turned her face to stone,
her curly hair to snakes,

and her tongue dried up
trying to escape her children.
We skated her surface,
the old ice pond

with its treacherous
depths and greenish patches.
When she melted for moments
she touched my cheek, snowflake,

like a hot penny
burning a hole to my heart.
In her inward chill
I seared myself over,

a young girl
skating away, writing
on air
with a red muffler.

Her silence; my silence:
the house, its stubborn necessities;
the snow, her scabbed
depression, drifted secretly

till even the blades of our
ice skates stopped
their thin persistent scraping on
her winter; the knife sharp air.

Kathleen Spivack

My Mother's Breakfront

She acquired an eye
for cracks and chips
bargained down the price
the plates were flawed
but hers
and when she turned
the damage to the wall
they looked intact

when I die
these pieces
are for you

Janet Sternburg

My Mother and the Bed

no not that way she'd
say when I was 7 pulling
the bottom sheet smooth
you've got to   saying
hospital corners

I wet the bed much later
than I should, until
just writing this I
hadn't thought of
the connection

My mother would never
sleep on sheets someone
else had   I never
saw any stains on hers
tho her bedroom was

a maze of powder   hair
pins   black dresses
Sometimes she brings her
own sheets to my house
carries toiletseat covers

Lyn did anybody sleep
in my she always asks
Her sheets her hair
smell of smoke she
says the rooms here
smell funny

we drive at 3 AM
slow into Boston and
strip what looks like
two clean beds as the
sky gets light   I

smooth on the form
fitted flower bottom
she redoes it

She thinks of my life
as a bed only she
can make right

Lyn Lifshin

First Menstruation

I had been waiting
waiting for what felt like lifetimes.
When the first girls stayed out of the ocean
a few days a month, wore shorts instead of a swimsuit
I watched them enviously.
I even stayed out once in a while, pretending.

At last, finding blood on my panties
I carried them to my mother, hoping
unsure, afraid—Mom, is this it?

She gave me Kotex and belt
showed me how to wear it.
Dot Lutz was there, smiling, saying when her Bonnie
got her period, she told her
when you have questions, come to me, ask me.
You can ask a mother anything.

I felt so strange when she said that.
Mom didn't say anything.

The three of us
standing in the bedroom
me, the woman-child, standing with the older women
and the feeling
there once was a feeling
that should be here,
there once was a rite, a communion.

I said, yes, I'll ask my mother
but we all, except maybe Dot,
knew it wasn't true.

Ellen Bass ,

The Fish

I had about as much chance, Mother,
as the carp who thrashed
in your bathtub on Friday,
swimming helplessly back and forth
in the small hard pool you made for me,
unaware how soon you would
pull me from my element
sever my head just below the gills
scrape away the iridescence
chop me into bits and pieces and
reshape me with your strong hands
to simmer in your special broth.
You bustled about the house
confident in your design,
while I waited at the edge
imploring you with glossy eyes
to keep me and love me
just as I was.

L. L. Zeiger

The Survivors

Night after night
She dreamed we were drowned
Or covered with spiders
Or butchered or tortured

She took us all to bed with her

And woke up whimpering
And came to find our bodies
In the dark, brushing our foreheads
Sorting out our tangled limbs

Amazed to find us whole

By day her love for us
Was a prairie fire
That roared across our whole horizon
Burning us out of our burrows

"I touched the windowpane"
"I touched myself"
"I let the boys touch me"

Like small, crazed animals
We leaped before her
Knowing there was no escape

She had to consume us utterly
Over and over again
And now at last
We are her angels
Burned so crisp
We crumble when we try to touch

Judith Hemschemeyer

The Dirty-Billed Freeze Footy

Remember that Saturday morning
Mother forgot the word gull?

We were all awake but still in bed
and she called out, "Hey kids!

What's the name of that bird that eats garbage
and stands around in cold water on the beach?"

And you, the quick one, the youngest daughter
piped right back: "A dirty-billed freeze footy!"

And she laughed till she was weak,
until it hurt her. And you had done it:

reduced our queen to warm and helpless rubble.

And the rest of the day, baking or cleaning
or washing our hair until it squeaked,

whenever she caught sight of you
it would start all over again.

Judith Hemschemeyer

38 Main Street

sitting on the toilet
with you in the tub
Mommy Frieda May
the blue room like water
smell of wet clothes
and talcum you never
liked yr name Ben
couldn't come in
Sitting on the toilet
yr breasts floating
on the water you
younger than I
am now

Lyn Lifshin

Premonition
(in a voice my mother called "not your own")

It was Mama who was partial
to Aunt Viney, my father's sister.
It was Mama who first said
What about Jade?
when Aunt Viney had to go back
to the Byberry State Hospital.
It was the fourth time in half a dozen years.
It was Mama who said Uncle Harold
belonged there himself
because all his people was peculiar
especially his mother who was Sanctified
and didn't eat pork or nothing
and didn't believe in doctors or anything
just like my father's mother (and most of his people)
and such a house
couldn't be no good for the child.
So it was Mama
who first took pity
and not Dad.

If Mama came back from Mass
and found Aunt Viney
(who was on some kind of a probation
and living again with her peculiar husband)
and signified she could stay for lunch,
my father would get up from the radio,
leave the house without saying
more than hello
and not come back till past my bedtime.

Then he would have to warm up his own
dinner and get dressed
for the eleven o'clock shift.

But then Aunt Viney
had some kind of a relapse
and Mama went to get little Jade
out of that house
of old folks, Sanctified, and looking
like slaves. Making even that child
look old.
Mama dressed her up in my old clothes
which wasn't raggedy or anything
(Mama being so hard on me)
and we wasn't getting any help
from the court then.
And Mama coated her face with Noxzema,
to get rid of the ash.
And Mama combed and brushed her hair
as much as three times a day
because it needed
a lot of training.

But then we started getting help from the court,
and my father's brothers and sisters
started coming around.
They started getting very tight.
And Mama signified nasty about it.
But when they were gone, my father said
Don't push me, Evangeline.
Don't push.

Everybody knows Viney is the biggest fool
always crying, always crying and going off—
colored people got better things to do!
A grown colored woman making herself
crazy over the dead—plenty people die!
What she think she is—white?
What she got to be screaming for?
Mama is dead. Period.
And isn't she dead counting on God?

And Mama only said
that Aunt Viney was too young to be
so Sanctified
and she wasn't even
a bad-looking girl, at that.

Yvonne

The Contest of Nerves

Ma & I were at Louise's house
across the street again

I am so nervous these days Louise
Oh not as bad as me Girl

Ma & Louise
held their hands out
in front of them
over the rusty sink
to see who shook the most

Ma watched Louise's hands
Louise studied Ma's

I watched the shaking of each
accelerate

See Louise
mine are worse
No mine just look Eileen

By this time Louise
was motor powered
but Ma was revving up
and both were frowning now

I announced it was a draw
I was only five but knew some things

The shaking stopped
The subject changed

We had such fun in those days

Patricia Traxler

My Mother Was Always Dressed

She wore lipstick and powder
and her face smelled good.
one winter she wore a bearskin coat
and a purple hat from Guatemala
with a tassel.

the summer she wore a bathing suit
she stood me in front of her
and was photographed.
I look at us, squinting into the sun,
her body hidden behind mine.

once, in the gloom of the bathhouse,
I peeked at her naked.
her nipples were dark and alien,
and she smelled like soup.

Abigail Luttinger

In the Ocean

At first my mother would be shy
Leaving my lame father behind

But then she would tuck up her bathing cap
And fly into the water like a dolphin,

Slippery as bamboo she would bend
Everywhere, everywhere I remember

For though he was always criticizing her,
Blaming her, finding fault

Behind her back he would sneer at her
All through our childhood, to me and my sister,

She never spoke against him

Except to take us by the hand
In the ocean we would laugh together

As we never did, on land

Because he was an invalid
Usually she was silent

But this once, on her deathbed

Hearing me tell it she remembered
Almost before I did, and she smiled

One last time to think of it:
How, with the waves crashing at our feet

Having thrown ourselves upon her, for dear life
Bubbling and splashing for breath,

Slithering all over her wet skin

We would rub against her like minnows
We would flow between her legs, in the surf

Smooth as spaghetti she would hold us
Close against her like small polliwogs climbing

All over her as if she were a hill,
A hill that moved, our element

But hers also, safe
In the oval of each other's arms

This once she would be weightless
As guiltless, utterly free

Of all but what she loved
Smoothly, with no hard edges

My long beautiful mother
In her white bathing cap, crowned

Like an enormous lily

Over the brown arrow of her body
The limber poles of her legs,

The sad slanted eyes,
The strong cheekbones, and the shadows

Like fluid lavender, everywhere

Looping and sliding through the waves
We would swim together as one

In a rainbow of breaking foam

Mother and sea calves gliding,
Floating as if all three of us were flying.

Patricia Goedicke

Then the Skins Fall Apart

The fertilizer plant grinds fish into stink.
In the icebox a dove carcass cools while Moma
boils pumpkin in a castiron pot.

The house upfront is full of drying garlic
where you wait for the boy from Buras.
Riversand's soft as any barnbed.

You two roll in the garlic bulbs shaking the skin to pieces.
Moma stuffs shirts in starch clabber, twists them
into clubs and puts them aside for ironing.

After the first time you go home, helping
Moma fix supper. You wonder why this takes so long.
On your stomach the white scale of dried sperm,

you spit on it to get the smell. Moma presses
blouses, white dress shirts, the starch drying
under her nails.

You take a razor to cut the blister
school shoes give your heels, pitching
the skin in the river.

When the cold lasts too long, too hard, green
oranges rot on the limbs. The knot on your belly
turns in like a knot on a navel orange.

You wish your stomach would drop off.
You dice up garlic heads, their smell
like drying blood lasts all day on your hands.

Dara Wier

Burns

The cat brushes past
and the shade of the bronze lamp
leans against the bulb—
another brown flower
blossoms on the pale cloth.
I made this shade myself,
stitching the big, vague roses
of a cotton shirt onto a cone
of wire. Now smell it—
the laundry room, twenty years ago,
my mother staring
at the clouded window, the iron
sinking into linen, leaving
a black ship
that won't push off again.

Sandra Hoben

Tricks

My mother
the magician
can make eggs
appear in her hand.
My ovaries
appear in her hand, black as figs and
wrinkled as fingers on wash-day.

She closes her hand
and when she opens it
nothing.

She pulls silk scarves out of her ears
in all colors, jewels from her mouth,
milk from her nipples. My mother the naked
magician stands on the white stage
and pulls her tricks.

She takes out her eyes.
The holes of her sockets
fill with oil, it seeps up,
with bourbon and feces.
Out of her nostrils
she pulls scrolls
and they take fire.

In the grand finale
she draws my father
slowly out of her cunt and puts him
into a tall silk hat
and he disappears.

I say she can turn anything
into nothing, she's a hole in space,
she's the tops, the best
magician. All this

I have pulled out of my mouth right
before your eyes.

Sharon Olds

Color of Honey

mother's got salve
mother's got a way to go
mother's a sacristy
mother keep the germs away
protect us, mother
your little angel with cunt wings
mother, a big brain
mother, smarter than the little girl
mother, I must complete my solo
mother, I rebuff you
mother, I adore you
you're my true lover never fear
mother, I know I scowl I
don't mean to
see the starkness of morning, mother!
smell the sweet alyssum
here's my comely man to meet you
here's my lovely lady to see you
mother, the clams are all female
here's my saline self to mix with you
we're autochthonous
we're gathering wool
we're weaving a garment
we're very sophisticated
we don't need a try-out
we're combing the beach now
we're fixed stars we're binary stars
you're standing over me
you're standing behind me
you're standing by me

you're at my feet
you be my moon you be my
tormentor you howl at me
you lock me in my room
you keep me wise
you be my milk you be
my book, my tigress
my sparrow hawk, my steed
you correcting me
with your soft eyes
bright lipstick in a brown suit
color of honey

Anne Waldman

summer words of a sistuh addict

the first day i shot dope
was on a sunday.

                i had just come
home from church

             got mad at my motha
cuz she got mad at me.   u dig?

            went out.   shot up
behind a feelen gainst her.

             it felt good.
gooder than dooing it.   yeah.

              it was nice.
i did it. uh. huh.   i did it.   uh. huh.
i want to do it again.   it felt so gooooood.

       and as the sistuh

       sits in her silent/

       remembered/high

       someone leans for

       ward gently asks her:

          sistuh.

          did u

          finally

       learn how to hold yo/mother?
and the music of the day

           drifts in the room
to mingle with the sistuh's young tears.

       and we all sing.

Sonia Sanchez

Mothers

the last time i was home
to see my mother we kissed
exchanged pleasantries
and unpleasantries pulled a warm
comforting silence around
us and read separate books

i remember the first time
i consciously saw her
we were living in a three room
apartment on burns avenue

mommy always sat in the dark
i don't know how i knew that but she did

that night i stumbled into the kitchen
maybe because i've always been
a night person or perhaps because i had wet
the bed
she was sitting on a chair
the room was bathed in moonlight diffused through
those thousands of panes landlords who rented
to people with children were prone to put in windows

she may have been smoking but maybe not
her hair was three-quarters her height
which made me a strong believer in the samson myth
and very black

i'm sure i just hung there by the door
i remember thinking: what a beautiful lady

she was very deliberately waiting
perhaps for my father to come home
from his night job or maybe for a dream
that had promised to come by
"come here" she said "i'll teach you
a poem: *i see the moon*
       the moon sees me
       god bless the moon
       and god bless me"
i taught it to my son
who recited it for her
just to say we must learn
to bear the pleasures
as we have borne the pains

Nikki Giovanni

Poem for My Mother

Remember when I draped
the ruffled cotton cape
around your shoulders,
turned off the lights
and stood behind your chair,
brushing, brushing your hair.

The friction of the brush
in the dry air
of that small inland town
created stars that flew
as if God himself was there
in the small space
between my hand and your hair.

Now we live on separate coasts
of a foreign country.
A continent stretches between us.
You write of your illness,
your fear of blindness.
You say you wake afraid
to open your eyes.

Mother, if some morning
you open your eyes to see
daylight as a dark room around you,
I will drape a ruffled cotton cape
around your shoulders
and stand behind your chair,
brushing the stars out of your hair.

Siv Cedering Fox

from ***M****ourning* Pictures

Ladies and gentlemen, my mother is
dying. You say "Everyone's mother dies."
I bow to you, smile. Ladies, gentlemen,
my mother is dying. She has cancer.
You say "Many people die of cancer."
I scratch my head. Gentle ladies, gentle
men, my mother has cancer, and, short of
some miracle, will die. You say "This has
happened many times before." You say "Death
is something which repeats itself." I bow.
Ladies and gentlemen, my mother has cancer
all through her. She will die unless there's a
miracle. You shrug. You gave up religion
years ago. Marxism too. You don't believe
in anything. I step forward. My mother
is dying. I don't believe in miracles.
Ladies and gentlemen, one last time: My
mother's dying. I haven't got another.

Honor Moore

A Woman Mourned by Daughters

Now, not a tear begun,
we sit here in your kitchen,
spent, you see, already.
You are swollen till you strain
this house and the whole sky.
You, whom we so often
succeeded in ignoring!
You are puffed up in death
like a corpse pulled from the sea;
we groan beneath your weight.
And yet you were a leaf,
a straw blown on the bed,
you had long since become
crisp as a dead insect.
What is it, if not you,
that settles on us now
like satin you pulled down
over our bridal heads?
What rises in our throats
like food you prodded in?
Nothing could be enough.
You breathe upon us now
through solid assertions
of yourself: teaspoons, goblets,
seas of carpet, a forest
of old plants to be watered,
an old man in an adjoining
room to be touched and fed.

And all this universe
dares us to lay a finger
anywhere, save exactly
as you would wish it done.

Adrienne Rich

The Envelope

It is true, Martin Heidegger, as you have written,
I fear to cease, even knowing that at the hour
of my death my daughters will absorb me, even
knowing they will carry me about forever
inside them, an arrested fetus, even as I carry
the ghost of my mother under my navel, a nervy
little androgynous person, a miracle
folded in lotus position.

Like those old pear-shaped Russian dolls that open
at the middle to reveal another and another, down
to the peasized, irreducible minim,
may we carry our mothers forth in our bellies.
May we, borne onward by our daughters, ride
in the Envelope of Almost-Infinity,
that chain letter good for the next twenty-five
thousand days of their lives.

Maxine Kumin

Notes on Contributors

ELLEN BASS teaches writing workshops for women in Aptos, California. She is the author of *I'm Not Your Laughing Daughter* and *Of Separateness and Merging*.

HELEN CHASIN is the author of *Coming Close* and *Casting Stones*. She has been a Radcliffe Institute Fellow and Visiting Lecturer at the Iowa Writers Workshop. She lives in New York City.

LUCILLE CLIFTON has published several books of poetry, including *Good Times* and *Good News About the Earth*. She lives in Baltimore with her husband and six children.

BARBARA EVE REISS was born in Chicago and now lives in New York. Her poetry has appeared in *Esquire, Antaeus, The Nation,* and *The Agni Review,* among others.

SIV CEDERING FOX has published several books of fiction, nonfiction, poetry, and prose poems, including *Mother Is, The Juggler,* and *Joys of Fantasy*.

KATHLEEN FRASER was born in Tulsa, Oklahoma. Her books include *Change of Address, In Defiance (of the Rains), Little Notes to You From Lucas Street,* and *New Shoe*.

NIKKI GIOVANNI comes from Lincoln Heights, Ohio. Her books include *Black Feeling, Black Talk, Black Judgement; Night Comes Softly,* and *My House*.

PATRICIA GOEDICKE is the author of *For the Four Corners, Between Oceans,* and *The Trail That Turns on Itself*. She lives in Mexico.

JUDITH HEMSCHEMEYER, a music lover, teaches at Sarah Lawrence College and Queens College. She is the author of *I Remember the Room Was Filled with Light*, *Very Close and Very Slow*, and *Give What You Can*.

SANDRA HOBEN currently teaches creative writing at the University of Utah where she is working toward a Ph.D. in English.

SANDRA HOCHMAN writes novels, plays, films, and poetry. She has lived as professor, actress, bookkeeper, journalist, wife, mother, mistress, and tap dancer. Her works of poetry include *Manhattan Pastures*, *Voyage Home*, and *Earthworks*.

JILL HOFFMAN is the author of *Mink Coat* and *Jack Shall Have Jill*. She was a Guggenheim Fellow in poetry in 1974–75.

ERICA JONG is the author of several books of poetry, including *Fruits & Vegetables*, *Half-Lives*, and *Loveroot*. Her novels are *Fear of Flying* and *How To Save Your Own Life*.

SHIRLEY KAUFMAN lives in Jerusalem, Israel, where she translates the work of Israeli poets. Her newest book, *Looking at Henry Moore's Elephant Skull Etchings in Jerusalem During the War*, was published by Unicorn Press in 1977.

MAXINE KUMIN's latest book of poems is *The Retrieval System*. She was the winner of the Pulitzer Prize for Poetry in 1973 for *Up Country*. Her other books of poetry include *The Nightmare Factory*, *The Privilege*, and *Halfway*.

LYN LIFSHIN is the author of many books of poetry including *Upstate Madonna*, *Leaning South*, *Black Apples*, and *The Old House Poems, Plymouth*. She lives in Niskayuna, New York, and is working on a recording for Natalie Slohm Associates in Cambridge, New York.

AUDRE LORDE is on the English faculty at the John Jay College of Criminal Justice at the City University of New York. She is the author of *The First Cities*, *Cables to Rage*, and *Coal*.

ABIGAIL LUTTINGER is co-editor of *Gravida* and is putting together her first book of poems, *Good Evening*.

JUDITH McDANIEL is a feminist, writer, and teacher currently affiliated with Skidmore College.

JUDITH MINTY has published poems in *The New Yorker*, *Atlantic Monthly*, and *Poetry*. In 1973 she won the United States Award of the International Poetry Forum for *Lake Songs and Other Fears*.

HONOR MOORE's poems have appeared in *The Nation*, *Amazon Quarterly*, *American Review*, and *The Little Magazine*. Her play, *Mourning Pictures*, was produced at the Lenox Arts Center and on Broadway in 1974, and was published in its entirety in the anthology, *The New Women's Theatre*.

SHARON OLDS's poetry has appeared in *Kayak*, the *Beloit Poetry Journal*, and *Ms. Magazine*. She lives in New York City.

LINDA PASTAN's books of poetry are *A Perfect Circle of Sun*, *On the Way To the Zoo*, and *Aspects of Eve*. Her latest book, *The Five Stages of Grief*, won the Alice Fay di Castagnola Award.

MARGE PIERCY is the author of several novels, including *Going Down Fast*, *Small Changes*, and *Women on the Edge of Time*. Her latest book of poetry is *Living in the Open*.

SYLVIA PLATH was born in Boston in 1922 and lived in Devonshire, England, until her death in 1963. Her books of poetry include *Ariel*, *The Colossus*, *Crossing the Water*, and *Winter Trees*.

ADRIENNE RICH has written many books of poetry, including *Change of World*, *The Diamond Cutters*, *Leaflets*, and *The Will to Change*. Her most recent books are *Of Woman Born* and *Poems, Selected and New*.

SONIA SANCHEZ was born in Birmingham, Alabama. Her works of poetry include *Homecoming*, *We a BaddDDD People*, and *It's a New Day*. She also writes children's books and is working on a novel.

ANNE SEXTON was born in 1928 in Newton, Massachusetts. Her poetry has appeared in virtually every important literary magazine in the United States. She won the Pulitzer Prize for Poetry in 1967 for *Live or Die*. Her other works include *To Bedlam and Back*, *Love Poems*, and *43 Mercy Street*. She died in October 1974.

KATHLEEN SPIVACK's poetry has appeared in *The New Yorker*, *Harpers*, *The American Poetry Review*, and *The Nation*. Her most recent books are *Flying Inland* and *Swimmer in the Spreading Dawn*.

JANET STERNBURG's poems and essays have appeared in *Aphra* and *Ms. Magazine*. Her play, *What the Woman Lived* (written with Corrine Jacker), will be produced off-Broadway. She lives and works in New York City where she directs the poetry series at the Manhattan Theater Club.

GAIL TODD lives in Berkeley, California, and teaches at San Francisco State College. Her book of poems, *Family Way*, was published by Shameless Hussy Press. The daughter of Jewish immigrants, she grew up in a housing project in the Bronx. She is married and has two daughters.

PATRICIA TRAXLER's first collection of poems, *Blood Calendar*, was published in 1975. She is finishing a second collection, *The Glass Woman*, and making the final revision on a novel.

LIV ULLMANN is an internationally renowned actress and the author of *Changing*.

ANNE WALDMAN's most recent books are *Fast Speaking Woman* and *Journals and Dreams*. She lives in New York City and works with the Poetry Project at St. Marks Church in-the-Bowery and the Jack Kerouac School of Disembodied Poetics at Naropa Institute, which she founded with Allen Ginsburg in 1974.

DIANE WAKOSKI has published several books of poetry including *Smudging* and *Waiting for the King of Spain* from Black Sparrow Press.

DARA WIER teaches writing and American literature at Hollins College. She's published fiction in *Mississippi Review*, and has a recent book of poems, *Blood, Hook, and Eye*.

ELLEN WITTLINGER has been a poetry fellow at the Fine Arts Work Center in Provincetown, Massachusetts. Her poetry has appeared in *Aspect, Massachusetts Review,* and *North American Women Poets: A Trilingual Anthology.*

YVONNE is poetry editor of *Ms. Magazine* and a free-lance critic of the performing arts. In 1974 she received a National Endowment for the Arts Fellowship and a grant from the Mary Roberts Rinehart Foundation.

L. L. ZEIGER won a 1975 Fels Award for her first publication, a poem in *The Paris Review*. Her poetry has appeared in many magazines since that time, and she has won the Poetry Now Newcomers Award and the Small Press Tour de Force Award.

ACKNOWLEDGMENTS

We are grateful to the following poets, publishers, and copyright holders for permission to include the poems in this volume:

ELLEN BASS: "For My Mother" and "First Menstruation." Copyright © 1977 by Ellen Bass. Reprinted from *Of Separateness and Merging*, by permission of Autumn Press and the author.

HELEN CHASIN: "Telemann." Copyright © 1968 by Yale University. Reprinted from *Coming Close*, by permission of Yale University Press.

LUCILLE CLIFTON: "My Mama moved among the days." From *Good Times* by Lucille Clifton. Copyright © 1969 by Lucille Clifton, Reprinted by permission of Random House, Inc., and the author.

BARBARA EVE: "Scenario." Reprinted from *Prairie Schooner*, vol. XLVII, no. 2, by permission of University of Nebraska Press and the author. Copyright © 1973 University of Nebraska Press. "My Daughter's Ring" printed by permission of the author.

SIV CEDERING FOX: "Poem for My Mother," © Siv Cedering Fox 1976. Printed by permission of the author.

KATHLEEN FRASER: "Flowers," printed by permission of the author.

NIKKI GIOVANNI: "Mothers." Reprinted by permission of William Morrow & Company, Inc., from *My House* by Nikki Giovanni. Copyright © 1972 by Nikki Giovanni.

PATRICIA GOEDICKE: "Circus Song" and "In the Ocean" printed by permission of the author.

JUDITH HEMSCHEMEYER: "The Dirty-Billed Freeze Footy" and "The Survivors." Copyright © 1975 by Judith Hemschemeyer. Reprinted from *Very Close and Very Slow* by permission of Wesleyan University Press. "The Petals of the Tulips" printed by permission of the author.

SANDRA HOBEN: "Burns" from *The Western Humanities Review*, vol. 30, no. 4 (Autumn 1976). Reprinted by permission of *The Western Humanities Review* and the author.

SANDRA HOCHMAN: "Thoughts About My Daughter Before Sleep," from *Earthworks* by Sandra Hochman. Copyright © 1970 by Sandra Hochman. Reprinted by permission of The Viking Press and the author.

JILL HOFFMAN: "Her Sleep." From *Mink Coat* by Jill Hoffman. Copyright © 1969, 1970, 1971, 1972, 1973 by Jill Hoffman. Reprinted by permission of Holt, Rinehart and Winston, Publishers, and the author.